Real Lives
Incredible
Successes

Inspiring People Who Overcame Adversity

Lyn Coutts

BARRON'S

First edition for the United States and Canada published in 2018 by
Barron's Educational Series, Inc.

Copyright © Green Android Ltd 2017

All inquiries should be addressed to:
Barron's Educational Series, Inc.
250 Wireless Boulevard
Hauppauge, NY 11788
www.barronseduc.com

ISBN: 978-1-4380-5039-3

Library of Congress Control No.: 2017958536

Date of Manufacture: January 2018
Manufactured by: Toppan LeeFung Printing Co., Ltd., Dongguan, China

Printed in China
9 8 7 6 5 4 3 2 1

Please note that every effort has been made to check the accuracy of the information contained
in this book, and to credit the copyright holders correctly. Green Android Ltd apologizes for any
unintentional errors or omissions, and would be happy to include revisions to content and/or
acknowledgments in subsequent editions of this book.

Image credits: www.shutterstock.com: Ludwig van Beethoven © Georgios Kollidas,
Frederick Douglass, Thomas Edison © Everett Historical, Vincent van Gogh © Everett –
Art, Stephen Hawking © Martin Hoscik, Pelé © A. RICARDO, Michael J. Fox © Debby Wong,
Haile Gebrselassie © Maxisport, Richard Branson, Steve Jobs, J. K. Rowling, Serena and Venus
Williams © Featureflash Photo Agency, Nelson Mandela © Alessia Pierdomenico, Bethany
Hamilton, Oprah Winfrey © Kathy Hutchins. Library of Congress: Walt Disney © Alan Fisher,
photographer. Wikimedia Commons: Leonardo Del Vecchio © Luck1112, Harry S. Truman © U.S.
National Archives and Records Administration, Milton Hershey © Hershey Community Archives,
Helen Keller © Los Angeles Times photographic archive, UCLA Library, Mahatma Gandhi
© Unknown / public domain, Jesse Owens © Acme News Photos / public domain, Albert
Einstein © Orren Jack Turner / public domain, Howard Schultz © Photobra Adam Bielawski,
Harry Houdini © unknown/ public domain, Charlie Chaplin © unknown/ public domain, James
Dyson © The Royal Society, Ella Fitzgerald © William P. Gottlieb / public domain.

Contents

What is an incredible success?

A success is accomplishing a goal or task. But when that goal had appeared beyond reach, or simply impossible, then it becomes an incredible success. Often these staggering wins capture the imagination, respect, and gratitude of people around the world. But sometimes, they go unnoticed, overlooked, or even forgotten. In this book, you will learn of many incredible success stories and the men and women behind them.

Many of the names are very familiar, others less so, but all are equally deserving of having their achievements honored. Highly successful people are not superhumans—they have their own trials and tribulations and make mistakes like everyone else. But while we may give up when faced with a hurdle, they keep going. They know the road to success can be rocky, but they are not afraid to fail. They learn from setbacks and try again, and again, until they achieve their dream.

Many incredible successes have benefited humankind. For example, the discovery of penicillin and the campaigns that resulted in equal rights, independence, and the end of slavery. These successes affected millions of people, and continue to do so today. Even a success that is more of a personal triumph can inspire others. When Bethany Hamilton got back on her surfboard after losing an arm in a shark attack, her victory became a victory for humankind's ability to overcome and adapt. Success stories in athletics or sports, like those of Haile Gebrselassie or Pelé, bring respect. Hearing the music created by the deaf Beethoven is moving, while munching a Hershey Bar makes people smile.

Incredible successes come in many forms, but they all have one thing in common: they are achieved by people with passion, dedication, courage, and talent. These people don't look back—their eyes are firmly set on the challenge, and the goal.

Richard Branson

Born: July 18, 1950, Blackheath, London, U.K.

On Richard's last day of school, his headmaster predicted Richard would either end up in prison or as a millionaire. Richard was dyslexic and had not done well at school, leaving without any qualifications. Despite this, Richard became hugely successful, known globally for his business acumen, informality, and sense of fun.

Richard always wanted to be an entrepreneur and at 16 he and a friend set up *Student* magazine. Aimed at school and university students, it covered politics, music, and celebrities. Richard left school to put more effort into this venture. Tapping into the student appetite for music, he set up a mail-order record company that sold records for lower prices than the retailers. He ran ads for this business, named Virgin, in the *Student*, and soon the record business was more profitable than the magazine. The name Virgin was suggested by an employee because they were all new to business.

Richard's next step was to open a record shop, which was also called Virgin. One shop quickly became a chain of shops. A Virgin record label and a recording studio, The Manor, followed. Virgin's first release was Mike Oldfield's hit album *Tubular Bells* in 1973. Many big names followed including the Sex Pistols, Janet Jackson, the Spice Girls, and the Rolling Stones.

Over the years, Richard became an important figure in other areas, too, and today the Virgin Group has more than 400 companies in retail, music, TV and radio, broadband, finance, health care, and travel—even space travel. Virgin Galactic is developing space flights for tourists. The VSS *Unity* is very close to having its first sub-orbital test flight.

Richard is well known for his sense of adventure. In 1985, he attempted to cross the Atlantic Ocean by boat. The boat capsized, but he completed the journey the following year in Virgin Atlantic Challenger II. Richard holds several speed records for journeys by boat and hot air balloon.

He is involved in humanitarian work and social responsibility projects. The Virgin Earth Challenge invites people to develop ways of removing greenhouse gases from Earth's atmosphere. Richard donated over $3.3 million as a prize for the successful invention. He was knighted in 2000 for services to entrepreneurship.

Richard Branson

"My attitude has always been, if you fall flat on your face, at least you're moving forward. All you have to do is get back up and try again."

Steve Jobs

Born: February 24, 1955, San Francisco, California, U.S.
Died: October 5, 2011, Palo Alto, California, U.S.

The American entrepreneur, inventor, and co-founder of Apple was worth $1 million when he was 23. Two years later and aged 25, Steve was worth more than $100 million. His incredible success was thanks to hard work and an unerring ability to spot future trends. In 2007, Steve used an ice hockey analogy to describe this: skate to where the puck is going to be, not where it has been.

Steve was interested in engineering and electronics from a young age. When he was 13 he needed electronic parts, so he found the name of the Hewlett-Packard boss in the phone book and rang him up. This resulted in a summer job for Steve in the HP factory.

Steve attended Reed College in Portland, Oregon, but dropped out because he was concerned about how much his education was costing his adoptive parents. Instead, he attended only the classes that interested him without paying. He slept on friends' floors, collected the deposit money on drink bottles, and ate free meals from a Hare Krishna temple. Steve's interest in electronics eventually led to a job at Atari as a technician, fixing circuit board designs on arcade games.

The birth of the Apple company in 1976 resulted from a collaboration between Steve and Steve Wozniak. Working in the Jobs' family garage, the pair developed and sold one of the first personal computers, the Apple I. To finance the scheme Steve sold his van. The Apple I was a success and nearly 200 were sold to computer enthusiasts. A year later, Apple II became the first mass-produced personal computer. In 1984, the Apple Macintosh (Macintosh is a type of apple) was launched with its mouse and GUI (graphical user interface).

Steve left Apple in 1985 to pursue other ventures. He set up the NeXT software company and invested in computer-animated film company Pixar, later becoming its president. He returned to Apple in 1997 when it merged with NeXT. His clever marketing and close work with designers created other innovative Apple products like the iMac, iPod, iPhone, and iPad.

Steve died in 2011 and was buried in an unmarked grave in a Palo Alto memorial park. His "think different" philosophy revolutionized the technology we use today. And it is likely that Steve's ideas will be evident in the technology of the future.

Steve Jobs

"Don't let the noise of others' opinions drown out your own inner voice."

Nelson Mandela

Born: July 18, 1918, Mvezo, South Africa
Died: December 5, 2013, Johannesburg, South Africa

Rolihlahla Mandela was born into the Madiba clan. At school, he was given the white Christian name of Nelson. When he was 12, his father died. After hearing stories of his ancestors, Nelson knew he wanted to end oppression and racial segregation in South Africa.

In 1944, Nelson joined the African National Congress (ANC). This movement fought for an end to apartheid, which segregated black South Africans. Nelson organized civil disobedience campaigns against this discrimination and, not for the last time, was charged and taken before the courts. In 1952, armed with his law degree, Nelson and his friend Oliver Tambo set up Africa's first black law firm.

A 5,000-strong protest in a black township in 1960 resulted in the police shooting 69 protesters. Over the following days, public meetings and the ANC were banned and many people were detained. This event became known as the Sharpeville Massacre.

Instead of peaceful protest, there was a call to use arms and Nelson was asked to lead it. Despite not being allowed officially to leave South Africa, he did secretly leave in order to rally support from other countries. On his return in 1962, Nelson was charged and sentenced, but before that jail term could be served, Nelson and 10 others were charged with sabotage.

Facing a death penalty, Nelson addressed the court during the trial. His "I Am Prepared to Die" speech has become famous. In June 1964, he and seven others were given life sentences. Nelson spent most of the 27 years in the notorious Robben Island prison, off Cape Town. It was from a cell that Nelson started talks with the all white apartheid government. In 1989, the newly elected white president called for a non-racist South Africa. On February 11, 1990, Nelson was released and his "walk to freedom" was broadcast around the world. Three years later he received a Nobel Peace Prize. In 1994, white minority rule was ended and Nelson became South Africa's first democratically elected president. He was also the country's first black president.

Throughout his life, Nelson never wavered in his devotion to democracy and equality. He was buried in an ancestral plot in his home village.

Nelson Mandela

"I have cherished
the ideal of a
democratic and free
society in which all
persons live together
in harmony and with
equal opportunities."

11

Oprah Winfrey

Born: January 29, 1954, Kosciusko, Mississippi, U.S.

When Oprah was young, her family was so poor she wore dresses made from potato sacks. She overcame the poverty and disadvantages of her early years to become a successful broadcaster and then businesswoman and philanthropist.

Oprah was born in rural Mississippi to a teenage single mother who was dependent on welfare. When Oprah was six years old, they moved to inner city Milwaukee, Wisconsin, where her mother worked as a maid. Over the next few years, her mother had three further children and Oprah was sent to live with relatives. As a teenager, she suffered abuse, got into trouble at school, stole from her mother, and had a stillborn baby when she was 14.

Her father took charge of Oprah when she went to live with him in Tennessee. Her education became a priority and she became an honors student and joined the high school debating society.

She started working in local radio while at university and was co-anchoring the evening news at age 19. That Oprah would go on to become an interviewer and talk show host was evident very early on. Her grandmother fondly remembered a very young Oprah interviewing a corn cob doll and even the black crows sitting on a fence!

Oprah's broadcasts were often peppered with laughter or tears. This emotional style won her a daytime TV talk show that became incredibly popular. *The Oprah Winfrey Show* followed. Her interview technique and the way she drew confessions from her guests was revolutionary. Oprah's ability to get people to open up has been called "oprahfication." This TV show—the highest-rated talk show in history—ran from 1985 to 2011.

Oprah has also had success as an actor and film and TV producer. She was the first black female multi-billionaire. She uses her shows and films as a platform to raise awareness of certain issues.

In 2007, the Oprah Winfrey Leadership Academy opened in South Africa to give girls from disadvantaged backgrounds education and leadership opportunities. By 2012, she had given $400 million to educational causes via Oprah's Angel network. Oprah received the Presidential Medal of Freedom in 2013.

"Whatever has happened to you in your past has no power over this present moment, because life is now."

Oprah Winfrey

Ludwig van Beethoven

Born: December 1770, Bonn, Germany
Died: March 26, 1827, Vienna, Austria

Ludwig was already a successful German composer and pianist when he started to lose his hearing, yet he continued to write music until his death. Initially he used ear horns and other aids to improve his failing hearing, but toward the end of his life, by now almost completely deaf, Ludwig communicated with people through written notes.

Ludwig was born into a large family. He started learning music when he was five. His father pushed him to become a prodigy like Wolfgang Mozart, a prolific and successful composer of the time. Ludwig was taught by his musician father and by composer and conductor Christian Gottlob Neefe. It is recorded that the young Ludwig did not always like the strict regime of his musical training.

By his teens, Ludwig was composing and being noticed by those who would become his patrons, wealthy people who made it possible for Ludwig to devote all his time to music. Yet the road to success was not smooth. His father was an alcoholic and when his mother died, the 17-year-old had to provide for his two younger brothers. Two years later, Ludwig ensured that half his father's salary was paid to him to cover the family's needs.

At 21, Ludwig moved to Vienna to study. There, he gained a reputation as a brilliant pianist. He lived in Vienna until his death, aged 56.

By Ludwig's late 20s his hearing had begun to deteriorate, and in the last decade of his life he was completely deaf. The cause of his deafness is unknown, but it made performing difficult. In 1824, at the premiere of his Ninth Symphony, he had to be turned around at the end of the performance so he could see the audience applaud—he could not hear it. This marked almost the end of Ludwig's conducting and performing career.

However, he continued to compose symphonies, piano concertos, piano sonatas, string quartets, and operas. He sometimes did this by sensing the vibration of a note through a pencil clenched in his mouth with one end pressed to the piano's soundboard, but mostly he imagined the sounds in his head.

Ludwig is one of the most famous and influential composers. Two of his compositions were on the gold-plated records sent into space in 1977 aboard the *Voyager* probe. They represent examples of the highest musical art achieved by humankind.

Ludwig van Beethoven

"What you are, you are by accident of birth; what I am, I am by myself. There are and will be a thousand princes; there is only one Beethoven."

Thomas Edison

Born: February 11, 1847, Milan, Ohio, U.S.
Died: October 13, 1931, West Orange, New Jersey, U.S.

Thomas was a prolific American inventor who, despite humble beginnings and a hearing problem, had a massive impact on today's world. We can thank the "Wizard of Menlo Park" for innovations in lighting, sound recording, and filmmaking. Thomas was mostly self-taught and homeschooled.

His hearing problem was most likely an inherited condition, although Thomas said that it was caused when a conductor threw him off a train following a fire that Thomas had caused doing an experiment. Thomas was completely deaf in one ear and had only 20 percent hearing in the other. He had little formal schooling, and what he did have bored him since he could not hear the lessons. Instead, Thomas became an avid reader. This explains how he was able at age 12 to write and produce a newspaper, the *Grand Trunk Herald*, which he sold to the employees of the railway company.

Thomas's first job as a teenager was as a telegraph operator on the railway. He was trained for this job by the grateful father of a young child whose life Thomas had saved. Eventually, Thomas started working for the Western Union Telegraph Co.

But it was as an inventor that he made his name. Thomas's first patent was for an electric vote counter. He went on to register a total of 2,332 patents worldwide. One of them was for a quadruplex telegraph (an improved way of sending telegraph messages) and it was with the money he made from selling this that he set up Menlo Park. This was a research laboratory specifically set up to invent—the first of its kind.

It was at Menlo Park that Thomas developed a long-lasting electric light bulb. Other inventions that came out of Menlo Park were the phonograph (a record player), fluoroscope (an early type of X-ray), kinetograph (a motion-picture camera), and a battery for electric cars.

Thomas's inventions impacted everyday things like lighting, entertainment, and power distribution. He founded 14 companies. His Edison Studios (1894–1918) made 1,200 silent films, and General Electric became a household name.

Thomas received many accolades, but Inventors' Day, started in 1983, would have meant the most to him—it is celebrated every year on his birthday.

"I have not failed.
I've just found
10,000 ways that
won't work."

Vincent van Gogh

Born: March 30, 1853, Zundert, Netherlands
Died: July 27, 1890, Auvers-sur-Oise, Paris, France

Vincent's painting *Sunflowers* was sold at auction in 1987 for $39.9 million, breaking the record for the most expensive painting ever sold at the time. It is one of the most recognizable paintings in the world. During his lifetime, only one of his paintings, *Red Vineyard at Arles*, was sold. Vincent's fame followed his death. His tragic story is one of misunderstood genius.

After failing at several jobs, including working for an art dealer and teaching at a school in Ramsgate, U.K., Vincent, aged 27, decided to become an artist. Supported by his younger brother, Theo, with whom he was very close, he moved around Europe and taught himself to draw and paint. These were hard times for Vincent. He was lonely and unhappy and his work was constantly rejected.

The art favored at the time was impressionism, with artists such as Claude Monet and Pierre-Auguste Renoir. The impressionist style was light and bright and tried to give an impression of a moment. Artists like Paul Gauguin reacted against impressionism and created bolder work. In 1886 Vincent, now living in Paris with Theo, was inspired by this movement. However, Vincent's paintings were even more expressive. He used thick paint, visible brushstrokes, and strong colors, but his work was still being rejected.

Vincent's life was characterized by periods of idleness and depression followed by frantic artistic activity. He spent time in psychiatric hospitals.

In 1888, he moved to Provence in the south of France and created the *Sunflowers* series of paintings. This was a productive time for Vincent, but he was also mentally unstable. One night when Paul Gauguin was staying with Vincent, Vincent threatened him with a razor. Afterward, feeling guilty, Vincent cut off the lower part of his left ear. He then checked himself into a psychiatric hospital with no memory of what had happened.

Vincent created more than 2,000 artworks in 10 years, lived in poverty, was considered "mad," and enjoyed no critical success during his lifetime. In 1890, he shot himself and died two days later. Yet just a few years after his death, his enormous talent was finally recognized. Vincent's dedication to his art and his harrowing story inspires people and reminds us of the importance of self-belief.

Vincent van Gogh

"Real painters do not paint things as they are ... they paint them as they themselves feel them to be."

Frederick Douglass

Born: 1818, Talbot County, Maryland, U.S.
Died: February 20, 1895, Washington, D.C., U.S.

Frederick was born into slavery, but rose to become a hugely influential leader and activist in 19th century America. Using his voice, his pen, and his conviction, he battled to end slavery.

Frederick's mother was a black slave and it is thought that his father was her white slave master. He hardly knew his mother since she lived on a different plantation and died young. At eight years of age, Frederick was sent to Baltimore to be a servant. There, he was taught by his master's wife to read and write, but the master stopped the lessons. His view was that education and slavery were incompatible. Frederick secretly continued to teach himself and others to read and write and began to question and condemn slavery. The young Frederick had realized that literacy and freedom were connected.

Frederick escaped from slavery when he was 20. His escape was aided by Anna Murray, a free black woman. Disguised as a sailor, he boarded a train and headed to New York City. It was there that Frederick adopted Douglass as his surname, after a character in Sir Walter Scott's narrative poem "The Lady of the Lake." Frederick identified with the character's rebellion against powerful rulers. This new identity made it easier for him to hide from his master and, in his mind, it also marked his freedom. In reality he was not truly a free man until years later when British supporters bought his freedom.

Frederick became a preacher and was encouraged to become an anti-slavery speaker. Aged just 23, Frederick embarked on a speaking tour across America's northern states. This was followed by two years in the U.K. where he gave talks while continuing to evade recapture as a fugitive slave.

Frederick welcomed the American Civil War, which broke out in 1861 over the issue of slavery. He recruited black troops to the Union cause and advised the president, Abraham Lincoln, that they receive pay equal to white troops. After the war, Frederick continued to campaign for equal citizenship and for women's rights. Slavery was abolished in 1865.

Frederick wrote about his years as a slave in his powerful autobiographies. His message changed the hearts and minds of many people and helped bring slavery in America to an end.

Frederick Douglass

"I would unite with anybody to do right and with nobody to do wrong."

Ella Fitzgerald

Born: April 25, 1917, Newport News, Virginia, U.S.
Died: June 15, 1996, Beverly Hills, California, U.S.

Ella had a troubled childhood. Her unmarried parents separated after she was born. Young Ella moved to Yonkers, New York, with her mother. There, Ella earned money as a messenger for gamblers, picking up tips and bets. Her dream was to be a dancer.

In 1932, after her mother's death, Ella moved in with an aunt. At school, she played truant and was sent to a reform school. After two hard, cruel years Ella escaped, and at age 17 she was living on the streets, penniless and alone. But she still wanted to be an entertainer and when she chanced upon an amateur talent contest she entered—and won it. As she had stepped nervously toward the stage, Ella decided to sing and not dance. This was a life-changing decision!

Within a year, Ella was legally paroled (Ella was a ward of the state) to Chick Webb's band. Scat singing entered Ella's musical repertoire. Scat is improvised singing where the voice is used as an instrument. With Webb, she co-wrote her first hit song, *A-Tisket, A-Tasket* (1938), which sold one million copies and was on the charts for 17 weeks. Ella was famous.

Following Webb's death, Ella married a convicted drug dealer and hustler, but she had the union annulled soon after the wedding. Out on her own, Ella landed a deal with Decca Records and recorded hit songs with the Ink Spots and Louis Jordan. A stint at Verve Records followed by a tour with Dizzy Gillespie were positive career and life moves. While on tour, she fell in love with Gillespie's bass player, Ray Brown. The pair wed in 1947 and adopted a child born to Ella's half-sister.

The 1950s and 1960s proved to be Ella's time of critical and commercial success and she became known as the "First Lady of Song." *The Cole Porter Song Book* album of 1958 became a classic and Ella picked up two Grammys—the first African American woman to do so. In total, Ella won 13 Grammy awards, recorded 200 albums, and sold more than 40 million records.

Ella could sing anything—ballads, bebop, jazz, and blues—and she performed around the world with all the greats of popular music of the time. Suffering from worsening health problems she made her last public performance in 1991 at Carnegie Hall in New York.

Ella Fitzgerald

"It isn't where you came from, it's where you're going that counts."

Harry S. Truman

Born: May 8, 1884, Lamar, Missouri, U.S.
Died: December 26, 1972, Kansas City, Missouri, U.S.

Harry was the 33rd president of the U.S., serving two terms between 1945 and 1953. He had never planned to become president or even be in politics. Harry's poor eyesight meant he could not go to military college, and his family could not afford to send him to college. Instead, when 14, Harry worked as a drugstore clerk and then on the family farm. It was the First World War (1914–1918) that took him in another direction. In the National Guard, Harry—now Captain Truman and in his early 30s—was sent to France.

After the war Harry married Elizabeth "Bess" Wallace and became a county judge in Missouri in 1922. He gained a reputation for being efficient and honest. In 1934, he was elected to the U.S. Senate and for more than 10 years Harry worked toward lifting America out of the Great Depression. He attracted praise for his work on a Senate committee that aimed to cut military expenditure. The committee's work saved American taxpayers money and made a name for him.

By 1945, Harry was vice president to President Franklin D. Roosevelt, but just three months later Roosevelt died unexpectedly from a brain hemorrhage. In reaction to this, Harry said, "I don't know if you fellas ever had a load of hay fall on you, but when they told me what happened yesterday, I felt like the moon, the stars, and all the planets had fallen on me."

The plain speaking new president had a lot to deal with. The dropping of the atomic bomb on Japan, the start of the Cold War between the U.S. and the Soviet Union, and the Korean War all meant he received much criticism. However, he also won much support for his efforts to rebuild Europe after the Second World War, to contain communism, and to introduce the "Fair Deal" program on education, housing, health insurance, and employment. These policies helped him to win re-election in 1948.

Harry also worked for civil rights reforms after hearing of the abuse and persecution of African American military veterans. In 1948, his executive order made it illegal to discriminate on the basis of race for positions in the civil service.

Harry retired to his hometown. He was the third president to establish a library to preserve the books and items relating to his presidency.

Harry S. Truman

"It is amazing what you can accomplish if you do not care who gets the credit."

Milton Hershey

Born: September 13, 1857, Derry Township, Pennsylvania, U.S.
Died: October 13, 1945, Hershey, Derry Township, Pennsylvania, U.S.

By the time Milton was 13 he had attended six different schools. His family moved each time his father pursued a new "get rich" scheme. After fourth grade, his mother urged him to leave school and find a trade. His first apprenticeship to a printer did not go well. Milton found the work boring. But he enjoyed his second apprenticeship to a sweet-maker and it changed Milton's future.

Milton worked in Joseph Royer's confectionery shop in Lancaster, Pennsylvania, for four years. When he was 19, Milton decided to start his own sweets business. He opened a shop in Philadelphia, Pennsylvania, using $150 borrowed from his aunt. For five years he worked at this business, but it was not a success.

Milton moved to Denver, Colorado, to work with another confectioner. There, he learned about making caramel using fresh milk—something he would come back to later in his career. He started other confectionery businesses, but these failed as well.

Milton was not put off, and back in Lancaster in 1883 he specialized in caramels. They were a success. His caramels were sold across the U.S.

Milton, though, was not content. After seeing chocolate-making machines at the World's Colombian Exposition in 1893, he wanted to make milk chocolate and sell it across the country. At the time, chocolate was a luxury product, but Milton wanted to make it affordable.

In 1900, he sold his caramel business for $1 million and built an enormous factory that could mass-produce milk chocolate. He located his factory in an area with lots of dairy farms so he had easy access to the fresh milk needed. He made and sold his Hershey Bars in bulk to keep the costs down.

The Hershey Bar was the first product to be nationally marketed and it was a huge success. Other Hershey products soon followed. As the business grew, Milton built a town around the factory, called Hershey, where his workers could live. The Hershey factory made Field Ration D bars for U.S. troops in the Second World War, producing 24 million bars a week by the end of the war.

Milton and his wife had no children. He used his wealth to fund charitable projects, including the Milton Hershey School that continues to this day.

Milton Hershey

"*Business is a matter of human service.*"

Helen Keller

Born: June 27, 1880, Tuscumbia, Alabama, U.S.
Died: June 1, 1968, Easton, Connecticut, U.S.

In the late 19th century deaf and blind people and people with other disabilities were not thought to be able to live a full life or make any contribution to society. Helen was to change those opinions.

Helen was born sighted and with hearing into a wealthy family. An illness when she was 19 months old—possibly meningitis or scarlet fever—caused her to lose her sight and hearing. Although Helen was able to communicate a little and distinguish members of her family, the outlook for her was bleak. Helen was bright, but unruly, and spoiled.

Helen's mother wanted more for her daughter and in 1887 contacted the Perkins Institute for the Blind. As a result, a private teacher was arranged for the six-year-old. The teacher was a young woman called Anne Sullivan who would go on to stay with Helen for the rest of her life. Anne was also visually impaired.

Anne first tried to teach Helen fingerspelling and signs for different objects, but the youngster would get frustrated and angry. Helen simply didn't understand that every object had a name and a sign. One day there was a breakthrough. Anne took her student outside to a water pump and let the water run over one of Helen's hands while signing the word "water" into the other. Helen understood the connection between the object and the sign, and from then on she quickly learned other signs.

By the time Helen was 10 she had learned to read Braille, fingerspell, and use a typewriter. By 16 she had taught herself to speak. She was also able to "hear" speech by reading people's lips with her hands. At 24 Helen became the first deaf-blind person to graduate from college. Anne was by her side the whole time. Helen wrote her autobiography, *The Story of My Life*, at college.

Helen attracted attention because of her disability, and she used this attention to highlight many causes, from women's suffrage to labor rights and disability issues. She traveled the world as a political activist—she was a pacifist—and a lecturer, and challenged the stereotype about people with disabilities. Helen was awarded the Presidential Medal of Freedom in 1964. Helen died in her sleep, and her ashes were placed alongside those of Anne Sullivan who had died in 1936.

Helen Keller

"The best and most beautiful things in the world cannot be seen or even touched— they must be felt with the heart."

29

Mahatma Gandhi

Born: October 2, 1869, Porbandar, India
Died: January 30, 1948, New Delhi, India

Mohandas Gandhi was a newly trained lawyer when he was thrown off a train in South Africa for refusing to leave a first-class carriage. After finishing his training in London, Mohandas had gone to South Africa to start his career. South Africa was, at this time, racially segregated, and Mohandas was outraged at the treatment he and other Indians were receiving. He went on to campaign for the rights of Indians, and later black people, in South Africa.

In western India Mohandas was brought up to respect all forms of life. Because of this he was a vegetarian and unwilling to meet violence with violence. Instead, with an understanding of how the law worked, Mohandas engaged in civil disobedience (a refusal to obey certain laws). On his return to India in 1915, Mohandas used civil disobedience to highlight the discrimination that existed in India under British rule and to petition for India's independence from the British Empire. It was the first time civil disobedience had been used on such a large scale.

Mohandas spread his nonviolent message by speaking out, urging non-cooperation with the British rulers and boycotts of British products and institutions. He used hunger strikes to make people listen; his longest fast was 21 days. The clothes he wore were symbolic, too, representing traditional Indian attire. Mohandas was unpopular with the British authorities. He was arrested six times and imprisoned twice in 1922 and 1930. Mohandas gained the support of the Indian people who named him Mahatma, which means "great soul."

In the Salt March (1930), Mahatma and others walked 248 miles (400 km) to the sea to collect salt. It was a protest against the British tax levied on salt. The British responded by imprisoning 60,000 Indians for disobeying the salt tax law.

Mahatma worked to improve the lot of rural Indians with education and the development of cottage industries. He also wanted an end to untouchability, which forced millions of Indians to be treated as impure or less than human.

A year after India gained independence in 1947, Mahatma was fatally shot. Over one million people lined the funeral route, and he was cremated on a pyre. Mahatma is credited with inspiring countless people with his message of peaceful protest.

"You must be the change you wish to see in the world."

Mahatma Gandhi

31

Stephen Hawking

Born: January 8, 1942, Oxford, U.K.

Stephen was studying cosmology at the University of Cambridge in England when he started to have difficulty walking. He had already completed a physics degree at the University of Oxford. But his academic career looked to be over when Stephen's problem was diagnosed as motor neuron disease, a rare condition that damages the nervous system. Stephen was told he had two years to live. To take his mind off this, Stephen threw himself into his research.

Stephen's research in theoretical physics was about understanding the basic laws of the universe, a previously little understood area. Despite the challenges his health posed, Stephen, with Roger Penrose, was able to prove Einstein's General Theory of Relativity: that space and time would have a beginning in the Big Bang and end in a black hole. He also showed that black holes are not black, but emit radiation and disappear eventually.

Stephen's disease progressed much more slowly than his doctors expected. When he could no longer walk without help, he used a wheelchair. As paralysis increased, Stephen needed around-the-clock care. His speech also worsened and he became harder to understand. In 1985, an operation (tracheotomy) was performed to help him breathe, but it left him unable to speak. At first he could raise his eyebrows to choose letters from a board in order to communicate, but in 1986 he began to use computer-generated speech. Stephen used to operate this with a hand, but now the predictive technology is controlled by a single cheek muscle.

Stephen has not only conducted groundbreaking research, he has also written many popular books on science. The most well known of these is *A Brief History of Time* (1988). With his daughter Lucy, he has also written a science-based adventure series. In *George and the Big Bang*, particle collisions, gauge bosons, and quantum theory are explained.

As a young boy, he was nicknamed "Einstein" by his classmates. Little did they realize that Stephen would come to be regarded as one of the most brilliant theoretical physicists since Einstein. With over a dozen honorary degrees and a CBE, Stephen continues to travel widely and lecture. His research still drives him, as does his wish to make it into space. Stephen is proof of what can be achieved despite enormous physical barriers.

Stephen Hawking

"Look up at the stars and not down by your feet."

Pelé

Born: October 23, 1940, Três Corações, Minas Gerais, Brazil

Pelé's full name is Edson Arantes do Nascimento. His father was a soccer player, and he taught his eldest son to play the game. But the family was poor and the "ball" they used was often just a newspaper-stuffed sock. His friends gave him the nickname Pelé, and it stuck. It became famous when Pelé started amassing the 1,281 goals that would make him the world's top goal scorer.

Pelé played for youth teams, and in his teens played on an indoor field. Because the indoor game is faster, Pelé says it trained him to think and move faster. And because he was playing and beating adults, it gave him confidence. He signed his first professional contract in 1956 with Santos FC, and played for them until 1973 before heading to the U.S. to finish his club career. His 58 goals in 1958 still stands as a Santos record.

Within his first year at Santos, Pelé was on the Brazilian national team. After the 1962 World Cup, rich European clubs wanted to sign Pelé, but Brazil's president declared the forward "an official national treasure" to prevent his transfer out of the country. Pelé went on to win three World Cup titles—the only player ever to have done so.

His two most famous goals came in 1961 and 1969. The first was at the Maracanã Stadium against Fluminense. He ran the length of the field, eluding the opposition before shooting the ball into the net. It is celebrated with a plaque that says: "The most beautiful goal in the history of the Maracanã." The second was his 1,000th goal, the O Milésimo, from a penalty, also at the Maracanã.

As Pelé's fame grew and he set more records, his wealth increased. For a time during his career he was the highest-paid athlete in the world. Santos took advantage of his celebrity to tour the world, and at the same time Pelé became an ambassador for "the beautiful game." Beyond the goals, it was Pelé's passion and flair for the game and the joy he felt and gave when he played that mesmerized people. His yellow No. 10 shirt, worn in the 1970 World Cup finals, fetched over $208,000 at auction in 2002—another record!

Pelé is one of the greatest soccer players in history, and has received many awards, including Player of the Century, and he is one of the "100 Most Important People of the 20th Century." Pelé remains an inspiration for all fans of sport.

"Success is no accident. It is hard work, perseverance, learning, studying, sacrifice, and most of all, love of what you are doing or learning to do."

Jesse Owens

Born: September 12, 1913, Oakville, Alabama, U.S.
Died: March 31, 1980, Tucson, Arizona, U.S.

Named James Cleveland by his parents, Jesse was the youngest of 10 children. His family was part of the Great Exodus—the emigration of tens of thousands of black Americans from racist American southern states to more tolerant northern ones. The Owens family made their new home in Cleveland, Ohio.

As a young boy, Jesse worked so he could contribute to the family's meager income. A job in a shoe repair shop meant he could not do after-school athletic practice. Fortunately, his junior high track coach, Charles Riley, spotted his talent and coached him before school instead. It was at school that his initials, J.C., became Jesse—and the name of one of the greatest track and field Olympians of all time was born.

Jesse started to set records in junior high, and in high school he equaled the then world record of 9.4 seconds for the 100 yard (91 m) sprint. At university he had to live off campus and work to support himself—black students were not eligible for scholarships. When traveling to races with the university team he wasn't allowed to eat with the white athletes or stay in the same hotels.

Jesse started to compete at a higher level and in 1935 he entered the Big Ten Championship for American colleges. In one 45-minute period, and carrying an injury, Jesse broke world records for the long jump, 220 yard (201.2 m) sprint, and 220 yard (201.2 m) hurdles, and equaled the world record in the 100 yard (91 m) sprint.

The following year the Olympics were held in Berlin, Germany, where Adolf Hitler was in power. Jesse was the games' most successful athlete, winning gold in the 100 and 200 meters, 4x100-meter relay, and long jump. His achievements disproved Hitler's views on white superiority.

Back home, Jesse was given a hero's welcome and a ticker tape parade, but the racial discrimination continued. To make ends meet he worked at various jobs, saying "I had four gold medals, but you can't eat four gold medals."

Jesse was an inspiration to all athletes, especially black athletes. He had talent and drive in abundance. He was awarded the Presidential Medal of Freedom in 1976 and the Congressional Gold Medal posthumously in 1990.

"We all have dreams. But in order to make dreams come into reality, it takes an awful lot of determination, dedication, self-discipline, and effort."

Albert Einstein

Born: March 14, 1879, Ulm, Germany
Died: April 18, 1955, Princeton, New Jersey, U.S.

Today Albert's reputation is such that the word "Einstein" has become another word for genius. However, his early education did not indicate what was to come. Albert was not considered an especially bright pupil. He had difficulty speaking clearly, for example, but he was curious and fascinated by certain things, such as what caused a compass's needle to move. He discovered an aptitude for geometry and calculus.

Albert left secondary school at age 16. He had disliked school and had not gotten along with the teachers who considered him a disruptive influence. He planned to go to university, but initially failed the entrance exam. His knowledge of subjects other than math and physics fell below the required standard. Albert did eventually gain admittance and when, in 1900, he graduated from higher education he had decided that physics, not math, was his passion.

While employed in a patents office, Albert worked on his doctorate. He was awarded this in 1905, by which time he had four revolutionary research papers published. These papers—on the photoelectric effect, Brownian motion, special relativity, and the equivalence of mass and energy—kick-started his academic career. Albert's work would go on to become the basis of modern physics and quantum mechanics.

Albert is best known for his Theory of Relativity, and he came up with what is arguably the most famous equation in the world: $E = mc^2$. In this, kinetic energy (E) is equal to an object's mass (m) multiplied by speed of light squared (c^2). In 1921, he was awarded a Nobel Prize in Physics for his services to the field of theoretical physics.

When Adolf Hitler came to power in Germany, the Nazis labeled Albert's theories as "Jewish physics." They organized a campaign against Albert and there were death threats. In 1932, Albert gave up his German citizenship, ended his professorship at the Berlin Academy of Sciences, and emigrated to America. He took up U.S. citizenship and remained in America for the rest of his life.

Albert was ahead of his time. The theories he proposed have earned later physicists Nobel Prizes, and there are many brilliant people still working on Albert's ultimate "theory of everything."

Albert Einstein

"I have no special talents. I am only passionately curious."

Michael J. Fox

Born: June 9, 1961, Edmonton, Alberta, Canada

Michael discovered a talent for acting at an early age, and by the time he was 15 he was acting professionally in a sitcom called *Leo and Me*. A few years later he had moved to the U.S. for more acting opportunities and became known as Michael J. Fox. Diagnosed at the age of 29 with Parkinson's disease, he semi-retired from acting in 2000 and set up a foundation to find a cure for the disease that affects the body's motor system.

At the height of his career Michael enjoyed commercial and critical success. He starred in the long-running sitcom *Family Ties* between 1982 and 1989, which earned him three Emmy Awards and a Golden Globe. He was also an international film star, best known for his role as Marty McFly in the *Back to the Future* films.

However, in 1991 the Parkinson's diagnosis set the actor on a different path. Parkinson's disease affects movement, usually making its sufferers shake uncontrollably and/or experience muscle rigidity. There is no cure at present and symptoms worsen over time. Sufferers can be treated with drugs to help control their symptoms, but the drugs can cause side effects. They can affect concentration and memory, for example. This disease usually affects older people, but it can strike younger people, too.

As it became harder for Michael to hide his symptoms, he took on fewer acting roles, choosing less demanding jobs such as voicing characters like Stuart Little in animated films. For his later work, Michael continued to receive acclaim and, in 2009, won his fifth Emmy Award. In 2012, Michael appeared in the TV series, *The Good Wife*.

Since 1998, Michael's main focus has been campaigning for research into a cure for Parkinson's. The Michael J. Fox Foundation is now the world's largest nonprofit funder of Parkinson's disease drug development. Michael's celebrity has raised awareness about the condition and he has appeared in public, sometimes without medication, to show the disease's effects. Michael has said that he engages with the challenges of Parkinson's disease with optimism and humor. He has written three books, including *Lucky Man: A Memoir* (2002).

In 2007, *Time* magazine named Michael as one of 100 people "whose power, talent, or moral example is transforming the world."

Michael J. Fox

"My happiness grows in direct proportion to my acceptance, and in inverse proportion to my expectations."

Bethany Hamilton

Born: February 8, 1990, Lihue, Hawaii, U.S.

At 13 years old Bethany set out on the morning of October 31, 2003 to go surfing with her best friend, Alana, and Alana's father and brother. They headed for Tunnels Beach in Kauai, Hawaii, an area they were familiar with. Bethany was comfortable in the water; she came from a family of surfers and had been winning surf competitions since she was eight. She was expected to turn professional. But what happened at 7.30 a.m. on Tunnels Beach looked to change everything for this top surfer.

As Bethany was lying on her board with her left arm dangling in the water, a tiger shark attacked. The 14 foot (4.3 m) long shark bit her arm off just below the shoulder. Alana's father used a surf leash to stem the bleeding, and Bethany was rushed to the hospital. She had lost over 60 percent of her blood in the ordeal and her heart could not pump sufficient blood around her body to keep her vital organs working.

Despite the trauma, and just one month later, Bethany was back on a surfboard, teaching herself to surf again. At first she used a board that had been made specially for her. It was longer and thicker than a standard board and had a handle for her right arm. She taught herself to paddle twice as hard and to kick with her feet to make up for the loss of her left arm. Soon she had no need for the custom-built board.

One year after the shark attack, Bethany was competing in professional competitions, using a standard surfboard. And in 2004 and 2005, she won the National Scholastic Surfing Association competition. She also won an Excellence in Sports Performance Yearly Award in 2004, in recognition of her incredible comeback.

In 2004, she published her autobiography, *Soul Surfer: A True Story of Faith, Family, and Fighting to Get Back on the Board*. In 2011, a film of the same name was made. Bethany, a committed Christian, married a youth minister in 2012; they had their first child in 2015. She and her husband teamed up in 2014 for *The Amazing Race* and came in third place.

Bethany triumphed over a catastrophic event because of her faith, determination, and passion. She doesn't see herself as a victim. She's just another surfer, albeit a very exceptional one.

"Courage, sacrifice, determination, commitment, toughness, heart, talent, guts. That's what little girls are made of; the heck with sugar and spice."

Bethany Hamilton

J.K. Rowling

Born: July 31, 1965, Yate, near Bristol, U.K.

Jo Rowling was working as a researcher and bilingual secretary for the charity Amnesty International when, in 1990, she was stuck on a delayed train. She had an idea for a children's book so she scribbled it down to fill the time.

This was an eventful period for Jo—she changed her career, lived abroad, got married, had a baby, got divorced, and suffered the loss of her mother. At times Jo was depressed and anxious. She was living on welfare, had little money, and was looking after her baby alone. She moved to Scotland and continued working on her book. Writing longhand on scraps of paper, Jo would work in cafes while her daughter slept in her baby carriage.

She completed the manuscript in 1995 and submitted it to publishers. Rejection letters flowed in, but in 1996 an acceptance letter for *Harry Potter and the Sorcerer's Stone* arrived with an advance of $1,992. The editor warned Jo that the book would be unlikely to earn her enough to live on—sound advice that proved so wrong! The book was published in 1997 with a print run of 1,000. To prevent boys being put off by a book written by a woman, Jo chose a pen name: J. K. Rowling.

In the end, *Harry Potter and the Sorcerer's Stone* went on to win multiple awards and sell more than 400 million copies across the world. The final title in the seven-book series, *Harry Potter and the Deathly Hallows*, was published in 2007.

The series broke many records for the fastest selling books and have been translated into 65 languages. The success of the books was unprecedented, making Jo wealthy. She is reported to be the ninth best-selling author of all time.

There is much in the Harry Potter books that reflects Jo's life. Hermione Grainger is based on an 11-year-old Jo, and the death of Jo's beloved mother is expressed in Harry's feelings of loss.

Film versions of the books followed and Jo's subsequent work has included a play, *Harry Potter and the Cursed Child*, screenplays, and production work. She has also written for adults.

Jo is involved in child poverty and social inequality charities. She is a patron of the National Multiple Sclerosis Society—the disease that killed her mother after years of suffering.

J.K. Rowling

"It is impossible to live without failing at something, unless you live so cautiously that you might as well not have lived at all, in which case you have failed by default."

45

Howard Schultz

Born: July 19, 1953, Brooklyn, New York City, U.S.

In the late 1970s and early 1980s, Howard was working for a company that made coffee makers. He liked coffee, but after visiting a small Seattle shop that roasted and sold coffee beans, he became passionate about it. He quit his job and moved to Seattle. Howard joined that coffee roasting company, called Starbucks Coffee Company, as director of marketing in 1962. It was a company with just three stores.

Howard had an exciting idea about how to grow the company. In 1983 on a business trip to Milan, Italy, he had seen that there was a coffee bar on every street. Not only did these cafes sell good coffee, they were also places where people met up. Back in Seattle, he tried to persuade the business's owners to sell not just beans, but also coffee beverages, and create a similar kind of coffeehouse tradition. A pilot of his scheme was successful, but the Starbucks owners did not want to take the idea on permanently.

Howard left the company in 1985 and set up his own coffee shop, believing there was a market for good-quality coffee. It was difficult to raise the $400,000 he needed. "I spoke to 242 people, and 217 of them said no . . . It was a very humbling time," said Howard. *Il Giornale* (Italian for "daily") coffee shop finally opened in 1986. Some of Howard's funders included the owners of the original Starbucks coffee bean shop. When these investors decided to sell and concentrate on another business in 1987, Howard bought the Starbucks name and the shops.

When the company went on the stock market in 1992 there were 140 Starbucks outlets. By 2016, Starbucks was a global brand with more than 20,000 stores. It is credited with changing the way we drink coffee and socialize.

Howard has been praised for Starbucks's ethical policies, such as using fair-trade coffee and hiring military veterans. The Schultz Family Trust promotes employment for people aged 16 to 24 and supports veterans to settle into civilian life. However, this reputation—and those of other global brands—did suffer when tax issues arose in 2013.

Howard's is a "rags to riches" story of a working class boy with total faith in an idea and the ability to build a business with 250,000 employees.

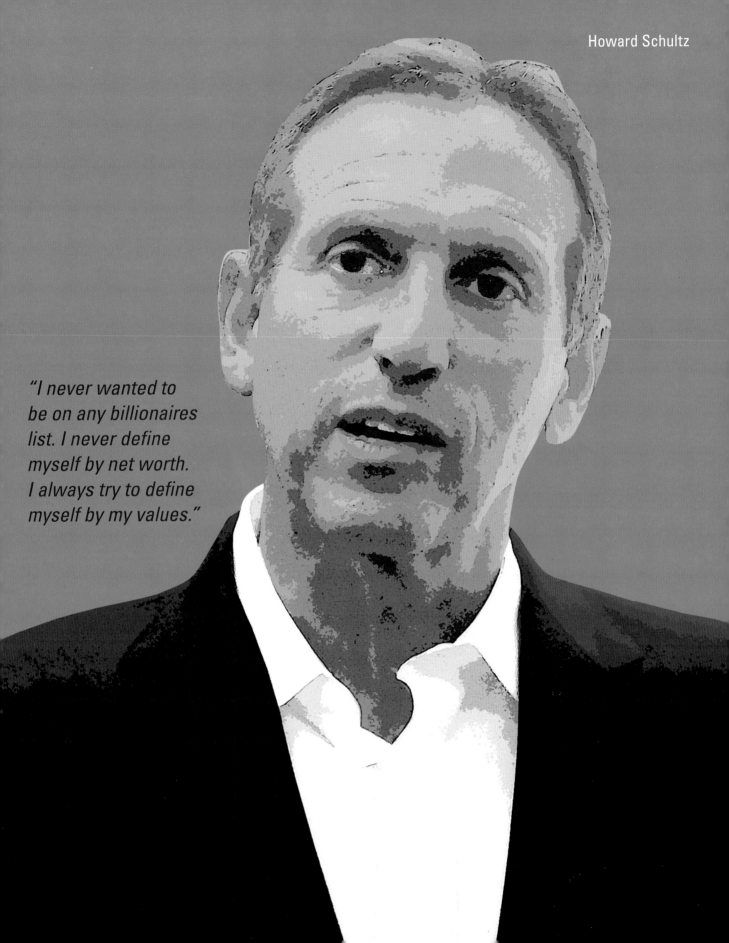

Howard Schultz

"I never wanted to be on any billionaires list. I never define myself by net worth. I always try to define myself by my values."

Walt Disney

Born: December 5, 1901, Chicago, Illinois, U.S.
Died: December 15, 1966, Burbank, California, U.S.

Walt, born Walter Elias, loved drawing as a child and he sold his sketches to friends and neighbors. When the family moved to a farm in Missouri, Walt cared for the farm animals—many of them appeared in his sketches and, of course, later in his celebrated animations.

Walt's father was stern. He used corporal punishment and denied his five children toys and treats. After two of his elder brothers ran away from home, Walt's loneliness, fear of his father, and a distant relationship with his mother further encouraged him to retreat into drawing and art.

At school Walt took illustration and photography classes and drew cartoons for the school newspaper. In 1917, he started art classes at night school. Rejected by the army for being too young to fight in the First World War, he forged his date of birth so he could help the war effort as an ambulance driver, drawing cartoons onto its side. His next jobs were as a draftsman and a newspaper artist.

By the early 1920s, Walt was making short animated films. Every frame was drawn by hand onto sheets of celluloid and then photographed by an animation camera. Despite some success, his Laugh-O-Gram Studio was bankrupt by 1923. A studio in Hollywood followed, which Walt set up with his brother, Roy. Hoping for commercial success, the Disney Brothers Studio created *Oscar the Lucky Rabbit*, which they sold to a New York film distributor. But just a few years later, Walt's Oscar character and many of his animators had been poached by a rival studio.

At rock bottom, Walt set about creating a new character. Mickey Mouse first appeared in 1928 in *Steamboat Willie*, the first animated cartoon to have synchronized sound. Walt did Mickey's voice until 1947. Mickey Mouse was a worldwide success and Walt created many animations of Mickey and his friends Minnie Mouse, Donald Duck, Goofy, and Pluto. Walt and his studio pushed the boundaries of animated filmmaking. In 1937, he released *Snow White and the Seven Dwarfs*, the first full-length, full-color, animated film. More animations followed, as well as live-action films and TV shows. Walt won 22 Academy Awards.

Although Walt has his critics, he remains the central figure in the history of animation.

Walt Disney

"If you can dream it, you can do it."

Haile Gebrselassie

Born: April 18, 1973, Asella, Arsi Province, Ethiopa

Haile had an impressive way of preparing for his successful future career as a runner, though he didn't know it at the time. He came from a large family that lived on a farm in Ethiopia and Haile had to run barefoot to school and back every day, carrying his schoolbooks. It was a 12.4 mile (20 km) round trip.

After so much training, but without any formal coaching, Haile took to running races like a natural, and he was quickly noticed for his long-distance ability. He won his first 1,500 meter race at school, despite being the youngest competitor. Afterward Haile said, "When we started the race, I went very fast and the other boys thought I would stop before the end. But I didn't."

Inspired to take running more seriously, and always focusing on long-distance events, Haile began his astonishing career as a track runner. At the 1992 Junior World Championships in Korea, he won both the 5,000 meter and 10,000 meter events. From there he went on to compete at the highest level in the World Championships and the Olympics. Haile has won eight World Championship titles and two Olympic Gold medals for the 10,000 meters. Later

he switched to indoor racing before focusing on road running with yet more success.

Haile earned a reputation as one of the world's greatest distance runners, racking up 27 world records. He has also broken 61 Ethiopian records. His road running is equally impressive—he won the Berlin Marathon four times in a row (2006–2009). In 2008, aged 35 (considered old for a runner), he broke his own marathon world record by 27 seconds.

Haile has worked as a mentor for G4S 4teen, which supports young athletes, and he was one of the founders of the Great Ethiopian Run. Haile still runs every morning and then goes to run his business in Addis Ababa, Ethiopia's capital city. He has built hotels and primary schools, operates a coffee plantation, and kicked off a local film industry when he built the city's first cinema.

Aware of the problems in his country, Haile's idea is: "If you want to help Africa, don't bring money. Rather, bring good ideas." Haile's early life may appear to have been disadvantaged, but look at what he's achieved for himself and his country—and it all started with that barefoot run to school.

Haile Gebrselassie

"When you run the marathon, you run against the distance, not against the other runners and not against the time."

Harry Houdini

Born: March 24, 1874, Budapest, Hungary
Died: October 31, 1926, Detroit, Michigan, U.S.

Born Ehrich Weisz, Harry was one of Rabbi Weisz and Cecília Steiner's six children. Ehrich was eight when the family moved to the U.S.

Harry began his magic career in 1891 with traditional card tricks. He billed himself as the "King of Cards," but fellow magicians thought him competent but not skilled and he had little success. He then began experimenting with escape acts. He met his wife, Bess, while performing with his brother at Coney Island, New York City. Harry and Bess married, and Bess was his stage assistant.

In 1900, Harry demonstrated how to escape from handcuffs at Scotland Yard, the headquarters of London's police force. This stunt got him a booking at the Alhambra Theatre in London and a wage of $300 a week. It was his big break!

Harry became widely known as "The Handcuff King," and he toured the U.K. and Europe. In each city, Harry challenged the local police to restrain him with shackles and lock him in their jail. In many of these escapes, he was first stripped of his clothing and searched. From 1907, Harry performed with great success in the U.S. He freed himself from jail cells, handcuffs, chains, ropes, and straitjackets. The tricks were often performed while Harry was suspended, upside down, by a rope above the ground.

With others copying his handcuff act, Harry dreamed up a new escape, from a large, locked, water-filled milk churn. The possibility of failure and death thrilled his audiences. One of his most notable stage illusions was performed at the New York Hippodrome, when he made a full-grown elephant, Jennie, disappear from the stage.

Harry was a true showman and astute businessman, and in his later years he uncloaked mystics and mediums as frauds. For most of his career he was the headline act and the highest-paid performer in American vaudeville.

Harry died of a burst appendix, and his last words were reportedly: "I'm tired of fighting." Harry's memorabilia, including the water torture cabinet and metamorphosis trunk, is housed at the International Museum of Conjuring Arts in Las Vegas, Nevada, which is owned by David Copperfield, the premier illusionist of this century.

Harry Houdini

"No prison can hold me; no hand or leg irons or steel locks can shackle me. No ropes or chains can keep me from my freedom."

Serena & Venus Williams

Venus, born: June 17, 1980, Lynwood, California, U.S.
Serena, born: September 26, 1981, Saginaw, Michigan, U.S.

Top tennis players Venus and Serena Williams began playing tennis when they were very young. They were not from a tennis-playing family. Their father worked as a sharecropper (tenant farmer) and came from a poor background. When he realized how much money could be earned in professional tennis, he decided that his two youngest daughters would become tennis players. But first he had to teach himself to play the game—only then could he start coaching his daughters, which he did on the neglected public courts in Compton, California.

As the girls' talent became clear, the family moved across America, to Florida. There, the sisters attended a tennis academy run by esteemed tennis coach Rick Macci. In 1995, after four years with Macci, their father once again took over the sisters' full-time coaching. Venus and Serena worked hard, putting in many hours of practice.

By the time she was 16, Venus made it to the finals of the U.S. Open, and her sister soon followed her. They quickly became known for their powerful performances and athleticism, and success followed success at the very highest levels of their sport. In terms of Grand Slams (the world's four major tennis tournaments of Wimbledon, the French Open, U.S. Open, and Australian Open), Venus has won seven, while Serena has won 23 Grand Slams—the most by any tennis player in history.

Though they are professional rivals, off the court the sisters' demonstrate closeness rather than competitiveness. Venus and Serena have suffered injuries and personal tragedy (their older sister was killed in 2003), and even encountered racism during competitions. Yet the sisters have remained at the top of their game.

In 2007, Venus campaigned for equal prize money for women in tennis. She argued that paying male players more than female competitors sent the wrong message to young players. Her crusade was successful and she was the first woman to receive equal prize money at Wimbledon that year.

The Williams sisters, with their dedication and inspiring rags to riches story, have had a massive impact on tennis and female athletics in general, breaking down prejudices about gender and race. Both women are still competing—and winning.

"Somewhere in the world a little girl is dreaming of holding a giant trophy in her hands and being viewed as an equal to boys who have similar dreams."

—Venus Williams

Serena and Venus Williams

Charlie Chaplin

Born: April 16, 1889, Walworth, London, U.K.
Died: December 25, 1977, Corsier-sur-Vevey, Switzerland

At the height of his fame, Charlie—a comedian, actor, writer, director, producer, and composer—was one of the highest paid people in the world and a global megastar. His Tramp character with his bowler hat, moustache, and cane is instantly recognized anywhere in the world.

Charlie had a tough start to life. His rags to riches story began in London. His parents performed in the music halls, and Charlie had already appeared on stage by the time he was five years old. But his father had started drinking and his mother spent time in mental institutions, and when his parents divorced, Charlie and his older half-brother were put in an orphanage. In the orphanage, the boys were poorly fed and they were beaten.

Charlie's professional debut was in a youth group, "The Eight Lancashire Lads," as a tap dancer. Later, at age 19, he worked as a comedian in Fred Karno's prestigious circus troupe, touring America. It was then that Charlie was spotted and was offered his first film contract.

Charlie made more than 30 short silent films with Keystone Studios, earning $150 a week, a huge amount at the time. In 1915, he started working with the Essanay Company, starring in and writing and directing longer silent films like *The Champ*, *The Tramp*, and *A Night Out*. People loved Charlie's blend of slapstick and sadness.

In 1918, Charlie built his own studio and produced and starred in *A Dog's Life*, which compared the lives of a dog and a tramp, and *The Kid*, a touching story of slum life. Charlie's early life clearly affected his work throughout his career. *City Lights* (1931) is a tale about a tramp's friendship with a drunken millionaire and blind flower girl, and it is regarded as Charlie's finest work.

Movies with sound (talkies) were becoming popular, but Charlie refused to use this new technology. This, along with his controversial political views, led to Charlie's loss of popularity. He left the U.S. and moved with his family to Switzerland where he worked on films up to his death. In 1972, he received an honorary Academy Award for his impact on motion pictures, and in 1975 was knighted by Queen Elizabeth II. Charlie's career spanned 75 years and he was a pioneer in cinema—perhaps one of its greatest.

Charlie Chaplin

"Life is really too short
to be insignificant."

James Dyson

Born: May 2, 1947, Cromer, Norfolk, U.K.

James was at art college studying interior design and furniture when he became interested in engineering and inventing. In 1970, James invented the ballbarrow—a wheelbarrow that uses a ball instead of a normal wheel. In the late 1970s, his attention turned to vacuum cleaners. He wanted to invent a cleaner that would not lose suction when the bag was clogged with dust. Over the next five years, James built more than 5,000 prototypes. Eventual success revolutionized the market.

James's inspiration for a bagless vacuum cleaner came after he saw how a local sawmill used large cyclones to remove sawdust from the air. This gave him the idea to use cyclonic separation for improved suction power. By 1983, he had made the G-Force vacuum cleaner, but no U.K. manufacturer or distributor was interested in James's bagless cleaner because they could make money from selling replacement bags.

Forced to look elsewhere, James traveled to Japan. There, he launched a reworked version. This vacuum cleaner was bright pink and functioned as a small table when not in use. The product won the International Design Fair Prize in Japan in 1991.

When James returned to the U.K. he was disappointed to find that manufacturers and distributors were still reluctant to take on his product. James decided to make and sell it himself. He set up the Dyson company in 1987. The advertising drew attention to the fact that it was a bagless cleaner. Customers were also hooked by the machine's efficiency and cool design. James's cleaner became the U.K.'s fastest selling cleaner, and was equally popular when launched in the U.S. To prevent his invention being copied, James had patented his design in 1986. In 1999, James successfully sued Hoover for using his patented technological improvements in their own machines.

Dyson continues to transform other technologies. One, the Airblade hand dryers for public toilets, uses a wall of moving air to "scrape" water from wet hands. This uses much less energy than those that use heat to evaporate the water.

James has won many awards for his innovative products. He was knighted in 2007 and awarded the Order of Merit in 2015. His company has invested millions in research and robotics, and employs over 3,500 engineers and scientists.

James Dyson

"Enjoy failure and learn from it. You can never learn from success."

Leonardo Del Vecchio

Born: May 22, 1935, Milan, Italy

Leonardo's father died five months before his birth. His mother could not support Leonardo, her fifth child, so handed him, aged seven, to an orphanage and the care of the nuns. When Leonardo was 14 he left the orphanage to get work in order to support his impoverished family.

Leonardo was apprenticed to a tool and die maker in Milan, and at night was studying industrial design. His training in making molds for car parts and glasses served Leonardo well when he moved to Agordo in 1961. Agordo is the home of the Italian eyewear industry. There, he founded Luxottica, which would design, manufacture, and distribute eyewear around the world.

In 1967, Leonardo started selling complete eyeglass frames under the Luxottica name. He constantly learned more about the glasses industry. He understood the importance of investing to guarantee quality products, staff training, and leadership techniques to keep costs down. In just a few years Leonardo had acquired the acumen that took other business leaders many years to master. He knew what he wanted to do and now he had the skills and vision to carry it out.

Leonardo used his manufacturing plant to make glasses for other companies, then bought a distribution business. Instead of paying someone to wholesale their glasses, Luxottica did it themselves. Further success led to more manufacturing plants, including one in the U.S.

At this time in the mid-1980s glasses changed from being a simple sight aid to a fashion accessory. Leonardo acted on this quickly; Luxottica released more styles more regularly, used well-known fashion designers to create eyewear ranges, and bought licenses to famous brands like Ray-Ban, Donna Karan, and Chanel.

Leonardo took his now highly profitable and high-profile company into the retail sector, buying Sunglasses Hut, Sears Optical, and more. The group is now the world's largest producer and retailer of glasses and lenses. It has 77,000 employees and more than 7,000 stores.

With only a high school education, Leonardo proves that it is not the letters after your name that count, but the passion in your soul, a willingness to learn, and an idea that excites you.

"If I'd started selling fruit, I'd be passionate about fruit."

Leonardo Del Vecchio

More Incredible Successes

The men and women in this book are a small selection of the many inventors, entrepreneurs, artists, musicians, authors, activists, and athletes who have been driven to achieve incredible success. Around the world, someone is pushing the envelope, thinking differently, or taking bold decisions on his or her road to success. Here are more incredible successes:

Brownie Wise

Born: May 25, 1913, Bulford, Georgia, U.S.
Died: September 24, 1992, Kissimmee, Florida, U.S.

Brownie invented a totally new way to sell—and the product she put into every home in the U.S. was Tupperware! Her idea was to sell it from her home, inviting women to a fun, social event where they could see for themselves how good the product was. She then enlisted others to host Tupperware parties. Her party plan was the first example of social network marketing, and Brownie was the first woman on the cover of a business magazine.

Jan Koum

Born: February 24, 1976, Kiev, Ukraine

Jan and his mother left Ukraine and emigrated to the U.S. when he was 16. Life in California started on welfare that was supplemented by his job as a janitor and his mother's babysitting. Jan attended college but hated it, so he taught himself computer programming and went to work at Yahoo. After quitting Yahoo, Jan went traveling, but in 2009, when Apple launched its app store, Jan saw an opportunity. He started developing WhatsApp—a free messaging application that is now used by over one billion people. In 2014, Jan and WhatsApp co-founder Brian Acton sold their company to Facebook for $19 billion.

Alexander Fleming

Born: August 6, 1881, near Darvel, Scotland, U.K.
Died: March 11, 1955, London, U.K.

The son of a farmer, Alexander moved to London at the age of 13 and worked in a shipping office. After he inherited some money, he trained as a doctor and became a researcher working on vaccine therapy. When mold had formed around a staphylococcus culture (he had left the culture in his office while on vacation), Alexander noticed that the mold had formed a bacteria-free circle around itself. He continued to experiment and, in 1928, discovered that the mold culture prevented the growth of the staphylococcus. He named the blue substance penicillin. This antibiotic kills or stops the growth of some kinds of bacteria within the body.

Amancio Ortega

Born: March 28, 1936, Busdongo de Arbas, León, Spain

Once a 15-year-old shop hand for a shirtmaker, Amancio is now one of the three richest men in the world. He is also a very private billionaire. Amancio set up sewing cooperatives with local women to make quilted bathrobes. He opened his first Zara shop in 1975. Amancio retired from his vast textile company (Zara by then had 6,000 shops) in 2011, but he still goes to the office every day to sit with his buyers and designers.

Do Won "Don" Chang and Jin Sook Chang

Do Won Chang, born: March 20, 1954, South Korea
Jin Sook Chang, born: July, 1963, South Korea

After emigrating from South Korea, the young married couple picked up various jobs in Los Angeles, California, to make ends meet. Neither spoke English, but Don noticed that the wealthiest people were in the fashion business. He and Jin opened their first Forever 21 store in 1984. There are over 600 stores, and it remains a family business with their daughters as creative directors.

Stephen King

Born: September 21, 1947, Portland, Maine, U.S.

Stephen and his older brother were raised by their mother after their father left when Stephen was two. After getting a degree in English, teaching posts were hard to find so he worked as a laborer to support himself and his wife. The occasional sale of Stephen's short stories to magazines boosted finances. His break came in 1973 when his novel *Carrie* was published and later turned into a film. His early fondness for horror can be seen in many of his books, but he has also written science fiction, suspense, fantasy, and nonfiction. His 54 novels have sold in excess of 350 million copies, and many have been adapted for film, TV, and comic books. His novel *The Shawshank Redemption* was made into a film, and ranked as one of the best films of all time. He is among one of the wealthiest authors in the world.

Bill Gates

Born: October 28, 1955, Seattle, Washington, U.S.

Often at the top of the world's rich list, the co-founder of Microsoft also tops the philanthropy list. With his wife, Melinda, their foundation has given $28 billion to improve the lives of young children and fight poverty in developing countries. This includes $8 billion to eradicate polio, and then to rid the world of malaria and measles. Their latest goal is to improve children's education. Bill and Melinda are turning over 99 percent of their wealth to the foundation, and their Giving Pledge has encouraged other wealthy individuals to follow in their footsteps. From Harvard dropout in 1974 to being awarded the Presidential Medal of Freedom in 2016, Bill has become one of the world's most influential people.

Franklin D. Roosevelt

Born: January 30, 1882, Hyde Park, New York, U.S.
Died: April 12, 1945, Warm Springs, Georgia, U.S.

The 32nd U.S. president took office during the Great Depression in 1932. He fought for social reform, brought the country through the Second World War, and established America's leadership on the world stage. Franklin became one of America's greatest presidents from a wheelchair, after suspected polio left him paralyzed in 1921. In Franklin's biography it says: "He lifted himself from a wheelchair to lift the nation from its knees."